CALIFORNIA II

CALIFORNIA II

PHOTOGRAPHY • DAVID MUENCH

TEXT • DON PIKE

GRAPHIC ARTS CENTER PUBLISHING COMPANY, PORTLAND, OREGON

CALIFORNIA II

1713—1784

"No service is too great, no service is
too small for the love of God and
man."

To the memory of Padre Junipero
Serra, whose sandaled footprints in
California's dust are its most enduring
monuments, this volume is respect-
fully dedicated.

Pg. ii:
Ocre starfish along
the Del Norte coastline,
Redwood National Park.

International Standard Book Number 0-912856-32-7

Library of Congress Catalog Number 77-77265

Copyright© 1977 by Graphic Arts Center Publishing Co.

P.O. Box 10306 • Portland, Oregon 97210 • 503/224-7777

Designer • Bonnie Muench

Printer • Graphic Arts Center

Typography • Paul O. Giesey/Adcrafters

Binding • Lincoln & Allen

Printed in the United States of America

Sixth Printing

A stroll through winter's first mantle of snow, Sequoia National Park.

Surfer flows gently with a surging Pacific breaker off Santa Cruz.
Right: An eternity of sun and fog, San Rafael Mountains. Pages 8 and 9:
Volcanic giant Mt. Shasta and Shastina at dawn above Grass Lake.

A spring advent of California poppies in Antelope Valley.
Right: The Merced River and Vernal Falls plunges 317 feet (96.62 meters)
over a granite ledge in Yosemite National Park. Pages 12 and 13:
Desert primose and sand verbena below Coxcomb Mountains, Mojave Desert.

Father Serra's mission, San Carlos Borromeo de Carmelo, founded in 1770, Carmel Valley. Left: A primal meeting place of land and water along the rugged headlands at Bixby bridge, Big Sur coastline.

The surging ebb and flow of the Pacific surrounds rocky pinnacles
off Monterey coastline along 17 Mile Drive. Left: Waves crash standstone
headland in grand spectacle from The Slot, Point Lobos State Reserve.

A telling design of the never ending conflict-harmony between sea
and land, the Monterey cypress, 17 Mile Drive. Left: A natural but eroded
sandstone form in The Slot, Point Lobos State Reserve.

A pink jellyfish roams the quiet waters of Monterey Bay.
Right: An ethereal surge and flow of the Pacific along the Monterey coastline.

A large January breaker sends sea spray skyward off
Santa Cruz. Right: Storm in Natural Bridges State Beach Park, Santa Cruz.
Pages 24 and 25: Live oaks in summer fields of Santa Rosa Valley.

Kennedy mine headframe and water wheel in the gold country at
Jackson. Right: State flower, California poppies, in Sierra Nevada foothills.

Wells Fargo stage rolls out of historic Columbia in the Mother
Lode country. Left: Memorable and nostalgic Episcopal Church in Sonora.

State Capitol building in Sacramento. Right: A summer sunset
along the Cosumnes River as it enters the Sacramento River in delta country.

A pleasant Sunday on the sands of Pomponio Beach, San Mateo
State Beaches. Left: Majestic redwoods, Sequoia sempervirens, stand amid
sword ferns as a splendid example of preservation of the grand
things in nature, along the trail in Muir Woods National Monument.

Above: Brown pelicans and blue mussel shell with sun's last glint.
Right: Chalk cliffs of Drakes Bay, Point Reyes National Seashore.

A solitary row of Monterey cypress separates a city stacked
upon itself, a wall to wall life that is San Francisco since the 1800's.

The quiet waters of a summer evening along Monterey coastline.
Left: Birdeye view into San Francisco Bay over the Golden Gate Bridge.

ALMOST PARADISE

". . . on the right hand of the Indies

there is an island called California,

very near the Terrestrial Paradise . . ."

It is a land of shimmering dreams, a repository of mythic expectations, a place set apart by golden riches, fertile earth, benevolent climate, and boundless opportunity. It is a legendary land of milk and honey that has tantalized the fantasies of ambitious dreamers from Spanish conquistadors to Dust Bowl refugees, and every shade of hopeful argonaut, pastoral prince, and crossroads capitalist in between. It has beckoned them all with the promise, if not always the substance, of a pathway to happiness and fulfillment. It is California, and for hundreds of years and millions of dreamers, it has been the place where Paradise begins.

California was born, fittingly enough, in the sensual imagination of a 16th century Spanish romantic novelist. About 1510, long before European adventurers and navigators had reduced the *terra incognita* of the New World to a known quantity, Garcí Ordóñez de Montalvo had rhapsodized in the exploits of *Las Sergas de Esplandian* that "on the right hand of the Indies there is an island called California, very near the Terrestrial Paradise . . ." It was named for its Queen Calafía, who ruled a wondrously bountiful land and a horde of Amazons armed with golden weapons who delighted in slaying their male captives after exploiting them. There is no accounting for taste, and without probing the darker recesses of the Iberian male mind, it is enough to note that *Las Sergas de Esplandían* was immensely popular; so popular, in fact, that when Cortéz mistook the peninsula of Baja California for an island lying to the west of Mexico, he promptly named it for Montalvo's fabled land.

The name stuck, even though time and exploration restored the island to the mainland and the dream of Califía to Montalvo's imagination. The name adhered through centuries of international politics that changed California's outlines and her ownership, and the mythic heritage has proved just as tenacious. Although Calafía and her Amazons no longer figure prominently in any pipe-dreams of happiness and prosperity, California has been, and will remain for many, "very near the Terrestrial Paradise."

Montalvo's prediction of "an island called California" was nearer the truth than geography can admit, for California remained isolated from the rest of the world during the Spanish dominion, and even after American enterprise and technology had eroded the physical isolation, California would remain singularly distinct from the rest of the American West. There is even a case to be made today that California is a place apart from the rest of the country and the world, nurturing a culture and a state of mind that, in the words of T. H. Watkins, has created "a social environment of incredible variety and often startling peculiarities."

The evolution of this place and state of mind called California began over 400 years ago when Spain laid claim to the region on the strength of Cabrillo's voyages and discoveries in 1542, and then spent 200 years trying to forget the bagatelle that dangled at the fringe of her profitable Mexican provinces. It was not until 1769 that Spain showed any official interest in the region, and then only because the threat of Russian and European encroachment loomed too large to be ignored. Gaspar de Portolá and Fray Junípero Serra began the settlement by establishing missions at San Diego and Monterey Bay, but in the course of 50 years the Spanish presence could show for its efforts only 20 missions, a combined total of pueblos and presidios that could be tallied on one hand, and less than 4000 non-Indian residents.

The reason was quite simple: California was a remote and distant island, isolated by distance and geography. Although blessed with ample coastline and a number of navigable harbors, the prevailing winds off California are southerly and persistent—any mariner seeking commerce with the *Californios* faced weeks of monotonous and backbreaking tacking to windward. An overland approach provided no easy solution either, as the mountains of northern Mexico and the deserts of the Southwest presented formidable obstacles to transport of bulky trade items. But distance and difficulty have never stopped merchants when a profit was to be made; unfortunately, the gold and silver that powered the Spanish dreadnaught of Empire in the New World had not been found in California, so there was little to coax men of commerce across the desert or up the coastline. The *Californios* retired to a self-sufficient, pastoral life that produced little for export beyond hides and tallow, and managed to make themselves happy on something less than a thriving economy.

The Spanish were probably the most aggressive, single-minded, unreconstructed treasure hunters the world has ever seen, and yet they failed to uncover California's gold—probably because the native Indians didn't find it for them. There was gold—enough to make the dream of Calafía's island a reality—but it was Americans who found it, and Americans who pushed a fading Mexican presence out of the way to get it.

Gold and American technology made California accessible: the promise of money waiting to be picked up off the ground has a way of eroding the most awesome obstacles, and California's wealth made it advantageous, even imperative, that the state be tied to the aggressive new nation muscling its way into the heart of a continent. Captains of American vessels suddenly found sailing to windward on a

Left: August cumulus clouds dwarf a peaceful world of two figures
along the sands of Drakes Bay, Point Reyes National Seashore.

regular basis worthwhile, and steamships soon alleviated the problem; the overland route, while still cumbersome for trade goods, was soon an eager river of humanity washing toward the golden shore; and once the gold was dug, the thriving new state so rich in other resources provided a powerful magnet for the transcontinental railroad.

California had arrived. It had produced wealth of its own, and drawn a healthy population of men and women with ideas, ambition, and determination. It had eroded the physical isolation that marked the early years under Spain and Mexico. It had cities, ports, and towns that would endure beyond the brief existence of the gold strikes, because the state had timber and agriculture and grazing to carry the boom forward. Although California had acquired most of the trappings of the burgeoning American nation and was no longer physically remote, the state would remain distinct from the rest of the west, truly an island at the edge of this great continent.

Part of what kept California aloof from the experience of other states in the trans-Mississippi West was a direct result of the gold rush and the sudden subsequent wealth. Unlike other western states, which saw much of the wealth generated by their natural resources drained off by eastern investors and absentee owners, California managed to hold onto a lot of the cash that was dug out of the ground and out of miners' pockets. This ready money became the capital that developed many of the infant industries and businesses that every new land must have, and also became the investment capital the Californians would sow in the emerging West.

By this means, California became a creditor, able to keep her wealth at home, and further able to reap the profits of a fertile West. Probably the most striking example of this principle in action is the Comstock Lode of Nevada, which created greater California fortunes than our own gold rush had. Tunneling after silver ore on the eastern slope of the Sierra Nevada was a costly undertaking, as was the reduction of the ore into silver. The money to pursue and refine the ore came largely from California, to which the silver eventually, and naturally, returned. This economic influence soon broadened to political domination, until it was suggested in many quarters that California was represented by four distinguished United States Senators, two of whom just happened to live in Nevada.

Creditor status seems a small point, even when all other western states were debtors, but it operated within a system where the creditors got richer and the debtors got manipulated. California was a winner from the beginning, with a winner's built-in momentum and self-confidence. California not only had no absentee landlords directing her affairs and draining off the profits, she was doing precisely that to other western states—always to California's advantage. George Hearst used profits from the Comstock to bankroll the Homestake Mine, dragging South Dakota gold home to lay the foundation for a family empire in publishing; Bank of America was California gold that became Comstock silver, that became thousands of lucrative investments throughout the West; and Tevis and Haggin (later Kern County Land

Company) used the same formula to eventually control hundreds of thousands of acres in California, and nearly a million and a half more in Arizona and New Mexico. The examples are legion, and they are by no means restricted to the past, but the point is that this situation was good for California: it gave the state the money to develop its own resources; it gave to each man a higher standard of living; and it gave to all a larger measure of control over the state's development and destiny.

California remained distinct from the rest of the west in another important respect—climate. California's sunshine is well-known and almost legendary, partly because there are a great many sun-bather days, and partly because no local Chamber of Commerce ever lets anyone forget it. An immigrant from Germany once lamented to me that he left his skis behind, because in all the literature his family had perused before departure, there was no hint of snow in the Golden State. Of course, that was before ski resorts had reached the level of development they enjoy today.

Sunshine by itself, however, is not enough; the Sahara has plenty of sun, as does most of the west, but neither supports the industry, the agriculture, or the burgeoning population that California manages to squeeze into its slender profile. Sunshine, to be effective and beneficial, must be tempered by an adequate rainfall, and here California departs from many of her western neighbors. Much of the west, particularly in the Great Basin, Rocky Mountain, and High Plains states, receives an average rainfall of less than 15 inches per year, the minimum amount for most kinds of unirrigated agriculture. There are local exceptions, and there have been wet cycles that raised hopes, but reliable, crop-raising precipitation has not been the region's long suit. Much of California, on the other hand, enjoys a Mediterranean climate of well-spaced gentle rains during the winter months (when evaporation is at a minimum and the moisture can be absorbed for the greatest benefit), and dry summers that range from mild to very hot.

With only a few exceptions, this weather pattern has been reliable, and the net effect has been to create a 500 mile long cornucopia in the state's great valley. Ample rains fall to water winter crops and grazing land, to restore the ground water, and to store moisture in reservoirs and the snowpack for summer irrigation. The long, hot summer provides a matchless arena for plant growth, without rain and hail storms to batter crops ripe for harvest. It is a condition that has built a vigorous agricultural industry that has become the single most important source of income to the state. California has delivered the most diversified range of agricultural products in the Union, and at the same time has nurtured large stands of timber that have kept the logging industry alive for a century and a quarter.

Sunshine and mild temperatures have likewise drawn other industries to the state, most notably movie making and aircraft manufacturing, which relied during their infant years on mild temperatures and an abundance of sunny days. People followed the jobs industry had to offer, but just as often the promise of what seemed like a life of perpetual sunshine drew an ever-increasing mass of humanity looking for a place to dally in idyllic splendor. I remember a time, not too many years ago, when graduates of a Rocky Mountain university would say they had found employment and were moving to Chicago, or New York, or Atlanta, or wherever; and just as many would say they were going to California, and figured something would turn up. They didn't even know *where* in California they were going; it was enough to be in that storied land because every bit of it, they were sure, had to be beautiful and bountiful.

Favorable press releases notwithstanding, California's climate can prove a little unnerving and confusing to new arrivals. Winter rains and summer drought seem like the natural order of the world to me and my family, because we are all members of California's largest minority, the native-born. But one day while driving through rolling hill country knee-deep in lush, green winter pasture, a friend only recently removed from his native Great Plains remarked with some agitation that everything in California is backward. "It's green in the winter and brown all summer, and that just isn't right." He had been stewing over this inconsistency that ran athwart his well-conditioned sensibilities ever since his arrival, and for a man raised close to the soil it proved to be too much. He returned to where the seasons turned like they should.

Unfortunately for California, his reaction was far from typical. Every year hundreds of thousands of people find that Montalvo's island is "very near the Terrestrial Paradise" for them too, resulting in a population growth that sets real estate men to salivating, chamber's of commerce to cheering, and residents to wondering if moats filled with flaming oil on the state's border would help to stem the tide.

California has a long history of extraordinary population growth; since the beginning of the American presence it has been axiomatic that the number of residents would double every 20 years. A more-than-healthy steady increase has periodically been stimulated into dramatic surges of growth by one tantalizing promise of good fortune after another. The Gold Rush transformed less than 10,000 into 224,000 in three years, settling most of them in San Francisco, Sacramento, and the mountain and valley towns surrounding the gold country. This population imbalance is still seen in the county lines drawn at that time; small, compact political units where the population was heavy, while the vacant reaches of the south state were accorded sprawling districts. The "cow counties" of Los Angeles, San Bernardino, and adjacent environs lunged toward equity with the land boom of the '80's, when California sun became a nationally advertised commodity, rail rates from Chicago dropped to a dollar, paper fortunes were made and lost every week, and housing lots brought prices that were still enviable in 1960. The Dust Bowl on the Plains brought another rattling exodus to the state in the '30's, when down-but-not-quite-out farmers brought their skill, patience, and hard work to a promised land that really didn't need them. The war sired two more phenomenal growth cycles: the first from 1939 to 1943 as a result of the aircraft and ship-building industries, and military

The branching trunk design of a California live oak, Marin County.

training centers; the second from 1945 to 1947 when the population leaped by another 1,000,000 as over 300,000 G.I.'s decided not to return to their former home, and brought their families out instead.

By 1950 California's population stood at 10,500,000, and has since grown to 21,500,000, an increase which represents an average growth of almost 1200 new people per day! Nearly 60% of those new additions were immigrants from outside the state, seeking something here they couldn't find anywhere else. There is certainly no sin in having the good sense to taste life on the Golden Shore, but unlike the loaves and fishes, California's resources are finite; as the quantity of humanity goes up, the quality of life must begin to go down. Because 90% of the population is urban, the problems bred by this galloping growth are most obvious in the cities, particularly in the San Francisco Bay area and the sprawling megalopolis that we once called Los Angeles, but which now threatens to link Santa Barbara and San Diego with an uninterrupted chain of humanity. In both urban centers the familiar problems of smog, traffic congestion, deteriorating core areas, over-burdened public utilities, and insufficient recreation facilities are obvious, and seemingly unavoidable. But growth and expansion of human endeavor are statewide, and some more fundamental problems are beginning to surface.

Water is a good example. California has been blessed with abundant water resources, and even though two-thirds of that water is collected in the less populated one-third of the state north of Sacramento, elaborate reservoir and canal systems have always managed to redistribute water to meet everyone's needs. This has been happening since 1913, when William Mulholland diverted the water of the Owens Valley and moved it 238 miles to keep Los Angeles growing. Californians have always managed to respond to the challenge, with the Hetch-Hetchy project to San Francisco, the Central Valley Water Project, and the stunningly impressive California Water Project which links the waters of the Feather River behind Oroville Dam with Los Angeles, and San Diego via the San Joaquin-Southern California Aqueduct. Although I have often been critical of these projects' methods and motives, I am at the same time humbled by the awesome engineering accomplishments involved.

But projects don't create water, they only move it, and the winter of 1975-1976 pointed up the fact that California is rapidly reaching its capacity to provide residents with a commodity as basic and fundamental to life as water. The winter was dry, and there were some of the expected hardships: winter pasture never matured, and grains and hay did poorly, hurting some farmers; cattlemen, as a consequence, got murdered on feed costs; and winter resorts had difficulty convincing the barrel-stavers that rocks and dirt made skiing more fun. But as droughts go it wasn't catastrophic, and everyone counted on reservoirs and always plentiful groundwater to pull them through the summer. The spring run-off, which rendered fishing an exercise in flailing muddy puddles, was a strong clue that some belt-tightening was in order, but many citizens failed to notice any crisis until mid-summer.

Farmers and ranchers began to irrigate early and often to make up for lost winter crops, and orchardists poured copious amounts of water onto the ground trying to maintain trees that rely on winter rains to establish the necessary six-plus feet of topsoil moisture. Demand by urban and industrial users had risen during years of normal precipitation because ample water made growth easy. Reservoirs that had never even been filled during the winter began to drop at alarming rates, because California had grown too big during the flush years. Cities had grown, industry had proliferated, and additional farmland had been cultivated, all on the strength and promise of water. One Sacramento Valley irrigation district was already at 100% of capacity; when the project was built, they were not projected to reach that figure until 1990.

The crisis became very real when several towns in Marin County north of San Francisco Bay saw their municipal reservoirs dry up, and potable water had to be trucked and piped into the system. As more towns faced the same fate, the residents responded like modern Americans everywhere; they screamed for the federal government to do something. Unfortunately, there wasn't much anyone could do because California's water resources were simply stretched too thin. Even the usually reliable ground water in rural areas began to get fickle: domestic wells that had never drawn down even in previous dry spells stopped flowing, largely because of numerous additional wells recently drilled into the same strata. Agriculturalists using canal water faced the very real prospect of having water cut off before the final irrigation, a circumstance that could have cost California billions of dollars in lost revenue and rising food prices.

Priorities became confused as businessmen, farmers, home owners, summer resort owners, and whole towns fought over the diminishing supply. In the Sacramento Valley, ranchers and towns wanted the water that ran by, but the delicate delta region needed a minimum level and flow to hold back the incursion of salt water. The delta could have been ruined, but then so could the thirsty towns and farms. The situation was saved by just enough water and an ingenious check dam hastily thrown up to divert fresh water to where it would do the most good in the delta.

Despite the fact that California survived the '75-'76 drought—and appears to have completely forgotten the lesson, although it can and will happen again—the consequences go far beyond a summer of hysteria. For example, when the rivers and lakes were drawn down to unprecedented low levels, water temperatures rose and oxygen levels dropped, both of which adversely effect salmon and steelhead spawning. Furthermore, gravel bars that provide traditional spawning areas were left high and dry, and when winter rains finally do come, those exposed bars will become heavily silted and useless. Migratory fish in California really did not need any more problems, but human need created another just as a matter of course. Wetlands for migratory waterfowl were similarly short-changed by the dry year, and because no water was available for diversion onto the fall feeding grounds, they are ripe for botulism—a prolific killer even in good years, and now a major threat to the entire waterfowl population of the Pacific flyway. Forty years of hard work and dedicated study by state and federal game managers, and private groups of hunter-conservationists like Ducks Unlimited, could be destroyed in a single year because plumbing is needed for 1200 new residents every day in Sodom-and-Gomorrah-South-of-the-Tehachapis. Somehow the exchange just doesn't seem worthwhile.

The implications for California's future that are reflected in her water problems are clear. The population is rapidly outgrowing the resources of space to move in, air to breath, a place to work, and a place to play. Despite all its advantages, California stands at the threshhold of super-saturation: a few more grains of humanity, and a once fluid solution suddenly solidifies. Too many people could turn even Paradise into just another factory for human activity.

It is impossible to say what draws them, for there are as many reasons as there are new residents. California offers unparalleled variety within her borders, an indiscriminate magnet for human ambition and activity. The state's 158,000 square miles encompass an incredible diversity of landforms, vegetation, weather, resources, and human activity, bound together by the expediency of political geography. California is the kind of place where the highest peak in the lower Forty-Eight, Mt. Whitney at 14,494 feet is scarcely 80 miles from Badwater, at 282 feet below sea level, the lowest point on the continent. It is a land that ranges from lush rain forest on the north coast, to the quintessential desert of Death Valley. California provides the arena for major mountain ranges and great valleys, broad rivers that stretch hundreds of miles inland before reaching the fall-line, world-renown cities pulsating with vitality, and small towns and mountain villages that move at a pastoral pace.

California lacks that single common denominator of terrain, or economic base, or ethnic heritage which so often ties others states together with the common bond of shared experience, but it is perhaps because of this diversity that so many people love her, and wouldn't live anywhere else on earth. For some, the essential California is the cosmopolitan grace of San Francisco, for others it is the high desert of Modoc County; to some, California is the broken coast of Eureka, or the oil fields near Bakersfield; others find their piece of heaven along the self-consciously beautiful shore at Santa Barbara, or amid the fundamental forces of the Mojave Desert; some know California as broad valleys that plow straight and deep, while others love her as pine forests that can give a lumberjack solace as well as employment; and there are many to whom the throbbing Los Angeles basin is the essential California, for one man's fault is another's blessing. California entertains a broad spectrum of human activity, largely because she seems to offer an endless variety of resources and places for man to practice life and living, but that fact tends to make her many things within one, and therefore difficult to know.

I have lived in California nearly all my life, rambling what I imagined to be her length and breadth over the course of nearly three decades. I played in her valleys and foothills during the normal mis-spent youth, and vacationed along her coast with my family; I came to know the northern Sierra and southern Cascades as only a hunter and fisherman could, lived in the state's forests working at disease control, drove heavy equipment in her agricultural expanses, and pursued Loreleis with summer-colored skin across the lotus land of Southern California. In the course of my work I have assayed California's history, both human and natural, and have worn out three vehicles researching and sight-seeing. But for all that, I still can't pretend to know the state—she is too large and complex a lady for one man to get his arms around, shifting her posture, attire, and visage as this grappler's vantage point changes. One supposes that therein, too, comprises a large measure of her charm.

For many people, residents and visitors alike, California is her coast. It is here that the outsider's dream of life in the Golden State often focuses, amid sunshine, gentle breezes, and relaxed outdoor living, lolling in a carefree stupor of sand and surf. This archetype of life along the Southern California strand is one that survives because in some measure it is true, although it has fostered some strange generalizations about the coast as a whole. Some years back I showed an adolescent youngster living in the Rockies my hometown on a map. Right away he wanted to know what kind of surfboard I preferred, and persisted with his question even after I explained that 100 airline miles and a mountain range separated my home from the ocean. I tried explaining that the only beach within three hours driving time had surf, rocks, and cliffs that would curl the hair on a kamikaze pilot, but he was undeterred, for he read magazines and listened to the Beach Boys, and he *knew* that everyone in California surfed. In his mind's eye California was sand from the Sierra Nevada westward, an unceasing pipeline of breakers curling from Crescent City to San Diego. He finally went away mumbling, convinced, I'm sure, that I either really didn't live in California, or was concealing some revolutionary new development in surfboard design.

Misapprehensions notwithstanding, California's coast is a wonderous thing of beauty and variety that entertains the libido and soothes the soul. It unreels for 1264 miles, through ten degrees of longitude, changing its aspect, climate, and even its personality with every mile. The far north coast, from the Oregon line south to Eureka and even Fort Bragg, represents a world apart from the blissful, sun-baked shores of San Clemente and Newport Beach. In the north the weather is a far cry from travel brochure idylls, with more than 74 inches of rain falling every year on Crescent City and chill winds a fact of life. Here, life is elemental and abrupt, where the ocean and the shore remind us that Nature is not always willing to succumb to the desires of men. It is a workingman's coast, where fishermen and crews on timber lighters have plied their trade for 100 years, fighting the storms and hazardous shoreline to earn a living, but ultimately accommodating themselves to the dictates of the natural forces.

The towns along the north coast often have a New England quality about them, with widow's-walk architecture and town-square planning transplanted along with the seamen who built them. The illusion is broken, though, by stands of giant redwoods (Sequoia sempervirens) that reach to cliffs which drop off into the sea. Unlike its southern counterpart, life along this coast is simple and direct, and hardly teeming with growth; fishing and lumbering have been in a long decline, and some of the towns are beginning to disappear along with the resources that once supported them. The coast retains its primitive aspect southward to the Golden Gate, although the weather mellows considerably this far southward, and thus far man's presence is largely restricted to the small ports and tiny coastal hamlets that have dotted the coast since the beginning of the American period.

Further south, in that great reach of shoreline between Monterey and Morro Bay, lies probably the most singularly dramatic piece of coastal landscape that California can call its own. Pinched down against the cliffs by the Santa Lucia Mountains, Big Sur has inspired superlatives in everyone who encounters it, and annually draws thousands of artists and craftsmen seeking an elusive commodity called inspiration in its thundering cascade of wind and sea. Big Sur has doggedly, and somewhat successfully, resisted the efforts of men to change its essential quality, while sharing abundantly of that quality with any and all who wish to pause and savor it.

At Point Concepcion the coastline turns to lie east and west, creating a shelter where Santa Barbara is tucked away like some delicate cachet. Protected on the north by the Santa Ynez Mountains, and to seaward by the Channel Islands, this narrow bench enjoys a climate approaching that of the Riviera. Man has tried to do his part as well, maintaining building codes and landscaping standards, resisting cheapjack development, and contributing time and money to preserving public edifices. Santa Barbarans have fought hard to restore the mood and appearance of the old Mission days, and have succeeded to such a degree that the downtown and beachfront areas exude an unreal, almost stage-set quality to those of us conditioned by typical California urban development. Once the retreat and playground of the very rich, Santa Barbara and the surrounding area have become more democratic, and as a consequence, more crowded. A great flap has been, and is being, raised over the drilling platforms, the oil spill, and the offshore refinery under construction, all admittedly undesirable additions to the region's scenic repertoire. But the area's growth seems an equally insidious threat to Santa Barbara's lifestyle. Caught between the abrupt Santa Ynez and the sea, there is a finite amount of room to accommodate the thousands more who arrive every year. Growth seems to be temporarily arrested because water is in short supply, but if the Santa Barbara arm of the California Water Project is ever completed, growth will once again leap ahead. Over the previous 20 years the leisurely, relaxed, neighborly way of life that once characterized this small corner of the world seems to have been disappearing, misplaced in the hurried intensity that has developed with the population. It is a condition that no one sought or wanted, but one that no building code or civic resolution can prevent. Santa Barbara is just too beautiful, and like many other places in California, it is being loved to death.

The renowned recreational beaches of the state have al-ways been those in the crescent of shoreline from Long Beach to San Diego. Years ago they were places for casual week-end outings, where children ran wild in the sand and breakers, discovering hidden worlds in Nature and themselves, while their parents basked in a haven from responsibility and temporal obligations. The ocean is still there, and so is most of the sand, but the ambiance that made a day at the beach something special got lost somewhere in the area's growth. Beaches where camping used to be a casual affair are now available on a reservation-only basis, and the rampaging hordes on the day-time strands rival those on the Santa Ana Freeway at 5:30 on any working day. As many as 2,000,000 people can hit the public beaches in Southern California on a big day like the 4th of July in an assault that makes D-Day look like a routine training exercise. Only a fraction of California's shoreline is public, but even if it were all public, every resident would only have four inches to call his own. I doubt if progress will ever completely annihilate the beaches of California; but more and more they are a hard place to have a good time.

There is another shoreline in California, gone now more than a quarter of a million years and discernible only to close observers, that delineates the kind of diversity the state provides for its residents. East of the Sierra Nevada the Pleistocene era created an immense inland sea nearly 100 miles long, that has since evaporated to become Death Valley. California never seems to do anything by half measures, and Death valley simply carries that tradition forward. Here in the skeletal remains of once-abundant moisture is land that makes no excuses for what it is, and offers no compromises to those seeking something that isn't here, for Death Valley is desert in its apotheosis.

At first glance it is a barren, bleak, monochrome of sun-baked earth and broken rock, where names like Hell's Gate, Dante's View, and Furnace Creek seem right at home. But Death Valley, like any desert, is a place of subtle enchantments that, once recognized, delight the eye and mind almost endlessly. Color changes constantly with every angle of the sun through a panoply of gentle and brilliant tones, until the senses seem they must be blunted to beauty, and then sunset and twilight put the lie to that notion, unravelling a whole new skein of wonders. Clarity pervades the desert, rendering sounds and scents almost tangible, and magnify detail until vision seems a recently regenerated faculty. Life becomes special and fascinating again where every living thing struggles near the brink of extinction, where plants and animals adapt or die. For the close observer every hillside, gully, and rockpile offers distinct circumstances where the live things of the desert seek moisture and nourishment by accommodating themselves to the environment. The desert invites close examination, but even for the casual visitor the broad vistas are worth a glance; and besides, there is something fascinating in the prospect of a land where life, including your own, is such a delicate commodity.

Death Valley is only part of the vast desert lands in the southeast corner of the state that lie in the rain shadow of the Sierra Nevada, San Bernardino Mountains, and the peninsular

Sedges live tenaciously in granites above Garnet Lake. Mount Ritter and Mount Banner, Minarets Wilderness in the Sierra Nevada range.

ranges of the San Jacinto, Santa Rosa, Vallecito, and Laguna Mountains. Pacific winds, sucked dry by these intervening mountains, seldom drop more than ten inches of rain per year on the Mojave and Colorado Deserts, and for much of the region four inches is normal. But despite the low precipitation, neither desert is a complete wasteland.

This desert quadrant was the bane of travelers through the 19th century, but during the last 50 years the region has grown more tolerable. Where once only solitary prospectors gophered their way through the desert, now a population of more than half a million find permanent homes, a figure that often swells five-fold on weekends. The dry conditions support only scanty vegetation, but the earth is rich in minerals, and large operations (with healthy payrolls) draw workers into the desert chasing borates, cement, potash, iron, and tungsten ores. Military bases dot the land, and the aerospace industry has moved into places like Antelope Valley. The more affluent have turned small desert oases like Palm Springs into winter playgrounds. And yet the sun-parched desert still predominates, bearing down with a dreadful aloneness on the solitary traveler, much as it did when immigrants crossed it on foot.

Twentieth century man has wrought a miracle of sorts in the Mojave and Colorado Deserts with the help of a little gravity and a lot of water. Irrigation has brought green islands to the sagebrush country, where incredibly rich soils and abundant sunshine combine to create vast open air hothouses—most notably in the Imperial Valley. Irrigation began to change the Valley almost immediately after Colorado River water was diverted to the area in 1901. In 1905 floods and faulty canals conspired to burst levees, and for two years the Colorado poured into the lowlands, creating New River and the Salton Sea. Today that same flow, although more controlled, irrigates almost a half million acres of cotton, lettuce, sugar beets, melons, carrots, grains, and livestock feed. Where once virtually nothing grew, the land now supports two crops annually in a year-round flurry of agricultural activity. It is big business, far removed from the Jeffersonian ideal of agrarian simplicity; but feeding the state is a big job.

The agricultural accomplishments in the desert are extraordinary largely because they are unexpected, but the real breadbasket of California is the great Central Valley. The Valley is California at its most prosaic, with no spectacular extremes of climate or landform, but these fertile bottomlands produce the crops that are an infinitely renewable economic resource; a resource that has held the state together through 125 years of good times and bad.

Nomenclature can be confusing for native and newcomer alike, partly because local preference and tradition vary from town to town. Geographically, the Valley is a 500-mile long depression, ringed by mountains, with one outlet at Carquinez; the northern portion, above the delta and the state capital, is called the Sacramento Valley, while the southern half is known as the San Joaquin. Up north in the Sacramento Valley the San Joaquin is often called the Central Valley, and inventive students have been known to allege three valleys between Redding and the Tehachapis: the Sacramento, the Central, and the San Joaquin. In fact it is but one valley, the Central Valley, with its northern and southern arms additionally named for the rivers they cradle.

The Valley supplies half the agricultural products of California, the state's single most valuable industry, in a variety that fairly boggles the mind. Historically, much of the southern San Joaquin was restricted to winter grains and grazing due to limited rainfall, but irrigation water now transported by the Central Valley and California Water Projects has broadened the variety of foods grown the length of the valley. Fruits and vegetables are commodities usually associated with California agriculture, from more pedestrian tomatoes and potatoes, to more specialized asparagus and melons, and oranges, peaches, almonds, walnuts, and grapes. But these represent only a fraction of the bounty that is harvested annually: cotton from the south-central valley, and rice from the north-central; alfalfa, barley, and wheat from peripheral lands all around the valley; olives from Corning and sugar beets from Yolo; peaches from Yuba and cherries from Stockton; figs from Fresno, and cattle from the entire basin. The list is endless and unnecessary, for virtually any crop can be raised in the valley, and at one time or another, someone has probably tried them all.

It has been a popular theme among writers on California to lament the passing of the family farm, complete with suitable tears wept for a vanishing way of life, in its stead we are learning to accept corporate farms, altering former family farm acreage into "factories in the field." There is no doubt that huge sections of land are being bound up under corporate entities, and that many holdings in the San Joaquin approach baronial proportions; which, incidentally, also describes California agriculture in the 19th century. On the west side of the San Joaquin, for example, nearly one-quarter of the 4,000,000 acres under cultivation are controlled by a handful of corporations. These are distressing patterns for California farmers, because land prices and operating expenses rise under this stimulus, while prices plummet with expanded production, but they do not sound the death knell for the family farm.

Narrowing profit margins have hurt the small family farm throughout the valley, and every year some are forced to sell, but everywhere many are holding on stubbornly. They remain not because the money is terrific, for most could realize an increased income by selling their land and investing the money in municipal bonds, but because this is the kind of life they want for themselves and their children. Farming and stock-raising demand long hours and hard work compounded by worry, but the life offers intangible freedoms and satisfactions found in no other livelihood. As long as there is dirt to plow, children to raise, and daily problems to challenge ingenuity, there will be men and women in California who would rather farm than be wealthy.

The Valley is more than farms, and few towns seem totally dominated by agriculture, rather their appearance is that of well-rounded communities with diverse economic bases just as elsewhere in the country. Many towns in the great Valley are growing at rates not justified by agricultural expansion, moderate-sized towns that offer neither big-money jobs nor big-city diversions. Recently it was discovered that California's major metropolitan areas are losing population, while the state continues to grow. A logical assumption is that many harried urbanites are moving to smaller communities, seeking something Los Angeles and San Francisco are lacking; in some cases, people are sacrificing lucrative salaries to earn a tenuous income where life marches at a different tempo. Maybe they're just looking for some good earth to sink their roots in; they could do worse.

Part of what makes the valley a good place to carve out a life is the ring of mountains which surround it, offering grand views and easily accessible respite and recreation. For those of us who grew up running the ridges, the real joy of California is her mountains. Time and age often play tricks on boyhood memories, but even if the days weren't all golden, and the adventures really didn't rival those of James Reddeford Walker and Jedediah Smith, the mountains were an unrivaled classroom for learning about the world and yourself, and a place of indescribable freedoms. Though it was many years before he realized it, the mountains of California taught one young boy that looking isn't necessarily the same as seeing, that frenzied activity does not always lead to accomplishment, that the world demands many kinds of courage, and that all men are not created equal. The joy came in learning this, and much more, while having a riotious good time.

California is ringed with mountains that cradle the entire great valley, and pucker the southern lowlands and deserts. The mountains of the south, principally the San Gabriel, San Bernardino, and Transverse Ranges, play week-end host to enormous numbers of people escaping the burden of city life, but the heart of California mountain country begins north of the Tehachapis.

The Coast Range points down the western edge of the Central Valley like a gnarled branch resting at the shoreline, worn by the elements. Even by the standards of geologic time this range is old, and it shows the effects of eons of wind, rain, and snow. The height and sharp definition of youth are gone, abraded by time into gentle contours. Because the weather cooperates by providing ample moisture and moderate temperatures, especially from the Bay Area southward, the range is dotted with valleys like Salinas and Napa that nurture delicate crops of lettuce, celery, artichokes, and grapes. Further north the range grows more impetuous and less benevolent, until it melds with the Cascade Range near the northern rim of the Central Valley.

California's most storied and well-known mountains are the Sierra Nevada, John Muir's famous "Range of Light." It helped to have publicists like Muir and Clarence King, but the Sierra would have managed without them. Here the '49ers dug the gold, and here most immigrant parties faced the final obstacle in their California quest. Here, too, are Yosemite, King's Canyon, and Sequoia National Parks, and the delicate jewel of the Sierra, Lake Tahoe. These mountains offer incredible variety, from low rolling foothills of oaks and brush, to the fabulous northern pine-growing slopes; from the giant trees of Sequoia National Park to the sparse vegetation of the more arid eastern slope.

The Sierra Nevada is the key to California's blessings, for it is these mountains that force clouds from Pacific storms high enough to wring most of the moisture from them. This condition leaves Nevada dry, but the abundant water caught on Sierran slopes is eventually tapped to keep California agriculture and industry healthy. These verdant forests also provide a year-round playground for Californians; skiing, camping, hunting, sight-seeing, back-packing, and fishing are all avidly pursued here, sometimes a trifle aggressively. Once the Sierra was a retreat, a place to restore the soul and recondition the body in splendid isolation, but in some instances the vacation population turns relaxation into a cheek-by-jowl confrontation. Yosemite now sports bumper-to-bumper traffic on selected week-ends, and hikers can tell horror stories of small tent cities rising in the back country; many campgrounds are forced to operate on a reservation-only basis, and then provide curbs, gutters, cinder block toilets, electrical outlets, and masonry fire-pits to effectively puncture every child's dream of emulating Jim Bridger. The primitive back country outside the parks is still there for almost every endeavor, but now it is a little tougher to find—and like most others who have found it, I'm not telling where.

In the far north, in the jumbled mass of the Cascades, are found yet uncluttered regions where the land and elements still dictate what man may and may not do. Stock raising and lumbering are among the few economically feasible pursuits, and they are not exactly boom industries these days. Here is a place to withdraw, to relive the glories of a mis-spent youth, and to show your children all the little live things of the mountain world at an unhurried pace.

The Cascades mark the southern reach of the Pacific "Ring of Fire," where spectacular volcanism created Mount Shasta, leaving her to brood over the whole region in glistening splendor. Lassen Peak is also a product of this process, but its presence bodes slightly more ominous—for it never saw fit to die, and periodically threatens to renew the activity that spewed ash and cinder from 1914 to 1916. Despite the past and the prospect, both loom like old friends over the northern mountains, landmarks in an era that threatens change.

The noted California geographer, David W. Lantis, once remarked of the Warner Mountains in the northeastern corner of the state, that "if this alpine fastness were adjacent to Los Angeles, it would be a nationally-known playground." Perhaps; but more than likely it would be a mess, over-run with a thundering horde, totally lacking in the solitude, wildlife, and untrammelled flora that make the Warners special. And that, succinctly, is the biggest problem facing the state. California offers extraordinary abundance, beauty, and variety, not only in her wild lands, but in every aspect of living. Yet too many people trying to share in the good life can, and do, strain the Golden State's capacity to provide adequately for them all. California is not a delicate organism, trembling at the verge of extinction; but for all her resiliency, the nearly 22,000,000 people trying to love her to death could end up being denied, or stalled somewhere short of Paradise and wondering why. The original Eden only had to contend with two people; perhaps even it would have suffered somewhat under this much pressure.

Despite all the glories of her wild lands and the good things to be found in her rural life, a realistic assessment of California must include her cities, for there is found the color and incessant range of human activity by which most of her residents know the state. Almost two-thirds of California's population lives in two major metropolitan concentrations: the San Francisco bay area, and the Los Angeles basin. The cities of San Francisco and Los Angeles are only fragments of the urban areas their names represent, but they provide the core around which a megalopolis can cluster. Each provides roots for the satellite cities of bedroom communities and industrial towns that serve and are served by them, and to a degree they provide an identity and personality for towns that, because of their youth and bland promise, would otherwise have little of their own. Whether one loves, hates, or tolerates them as a fact of life, both San Francisco and Los Angeles are the essential California for most of her residents, for they are home.

San Francisco has historically been the hub of the state's activity, dating from the halcyon days of the Gold Rush. Even during the 1860's, when a Californian spoke of "the City" everyone knew he meant San Francisco, a habit which persists even today among the natives. A long heritage of being the most beautiful, urbane, sophisticated, tolerant, and culturally edifying city on the coast has helped San Francisco to create a self-image of graceful living which moves at a relaxed cadence. From her skyline to her shoreline San Francisco is interesting and diverse, exuding charm in almost self-conscious doses, and creating an atmosphere of gentility and good taste. San Francisco was like a rich kid, born with all the advantages: a beautiful setting on rolling hills, complemented by a cool, even climate; blessed with one of the world's finest natural harbors; situated as the gateway to the treasure and produce of the rich interior mountains and valleys; and furnished with wealthy early residents who built concert halls and funded opera companies because a fine city ought to have refined diversions.

San Francisco's self-image is healthy, partly because it is true, and partly because it helps her partisans to resist the nagging suspicion that "the City" is no longer the city. A favorite past-time among California editors is promoting the rivalry between San Francisco and Los Angeles, wherein the city-by-the-bay smugly pokes fun at the "cow country" boors from Los Angeles, while Angelenos shrilly retaliate that Frisco is an aging, impotent husk of vanished glory with fewer orchestras, operas, theatres, and everything else, than the muscular young giant of the south state.

Los Angeles is, in many respects, the antithesis of San Francisco; a bustling hive of frenzied activity and perpetual motion, building up and tearing down, spreading across a coastal plain, never rising very high, but always reaching out in a concrete sprawl. Los Angeles built itself from a dusty cowtown at the outer orbit of the state's influence, into the center of population and commerce by dint of hard work. Perhaps representative of the city's energetic optimism is her port: where nature gave San Francisco the finest, she gave Los Angeles nothing, but the city built its own anyway, with pilings, and land fill, and concrete.

Los Angeles is raw energy and the ambitious ingenuity of man turned loose to do his best and his worst. I will never understand this rampaging metropolis, but I will likewise never get in its way. One of my earliest memories of Southern California is a Christmas visit with my grandparents. The gifts and goodies are only hazily recalled, but boldly imprinted on my memory is the image of my grandfather berating himself for not buying orchards in Orange County right after World War II. By 1950 Orange County was so obviously becoming House County that the favorite distraught diversion of longtime Angelenos was remembering the time they had an opportunity to invest in aging citrus groves for a mere pittance. My family was no exception.

The transformation of Orange County, and the entire Los Angeles basin for that matter, has been a fact of life, as irrevocable as any law of physics, for my entire life. It was an inevitability that might cause occasional teeth-gnashing by investors who were left out, but it was most often a source of dry wit and shoulder shrugging; it was going to happen, and there wasn't anything that anyone could do about it. The growth and sprawl was all just part of that glorious, entertaining, wealth-generating, smoke covered, sunshine laden, freeway riven, flower covered mess that Los Angeles was becoming and would continue to be. Mostly we just laughed, because there didn't seem anything else to do.

Los Angeles has grown into the force that governs California, both politically and economically, largely on the strength of population. This growth has been possible because Angelenos very early developed a cavalier regard for resources. When they needed water to grow, they took the Owens Valley's; when they needed more, they took the Colorado River's; and when they needed still more, they ventured north. The urban area grew, creating jobs, wealth, and progress, and that was justification enough for any action. The attitude is not malicious, just energetic and aggressive, like the city itself.

Los Angeles is an extraordinary phenomenon, nurturing the whole spectrum of the human comedy from the bizarre to the mundane. It provides a home for radicals and reactionaries, cultists and pantheists; from its fertile soil grew the drive-in restaurant, the drive-in movie, and the drive-in church service; it is a trend-setter in music, art, fashion, and lifestyle; it creates and markets celluloid fantasies, while harboring an aerospace industry whose technical developments outstrip the imaginations of script writers; and it is also a great many plain folks just trying to get by.

Los Angeles is the California that grew up in the last three decades. It was uninhibited, inventive, and apparently invincible, seeming to succeed at everything it ventured. Los Angeles became, and continues to be, an exciting experience on the frontiers of California's tomorrow, because one can seldom escape the feeling that this major metropolis may be a harbinger of that state's future.

Perhaps that is a possibility we should all consider.

A large sculptured driftwood and the Gold Bluffs of Redwood National
Park. Left: A siltstone arch at Table Rock Cove, Santa Cruz coastline.

Wild rhododendron blooms among fog shrouded coastal redwoods, reminder
of a primordial past. Right: Towering skyward, Redwood National Park.

Sonoma coast headland beyond the rustic fence at Fort Ross State
Historic Park. Right: Abstract sandstone forms, Sand Point State Park.

Summer fogs shroud Sitka spruce and the Del Norte coastal headland
along Yurok trail, Redwood National Park. Left: Reconstructed Chapel
at the 1812 Russian outpost of Fort Ross State Historic Park.

Leafing out of spring green accents coastal foothills and meadows
above Fort Bragg. Left: Profile of the Pacific and town of Mendocino.

California gulls soar in a never ending search for food along the
north coast tidelands. Left: Patient smelt fishermen try for a
mid-summer catch along the Mendocino coast north of Fort Bragg.

63

Stark reminders of ancient coastal scenes, Jedediah Smith Redwoods.
Right: Sunset along the Del Norte coastline, Redwood National Park.

Drifting mists veil giant redwoods above Redwood Creek, Redwood
National Park. Right: Rocky seastacks off shore at Trinidad Head.

In full bloom, large mounds of yellow and blue lupine strike exciting
colors and moods to May along the windy shoreline at Crescent City.

Volcanic Lassen Peak reflects into Manzanita Lake. Left: Design
of Jeffery pine cones on cinders in Lassen Volcanic National Park.

A generous assortment of young evergreens grow skyward below Sierra
Buttes, Sierra Nevada range north. Left: Snow geese in flight fill
the winter skies above Tule Lake National Wildlife Refuge.

A space-time tangency of the sun and Cinder Butte in Lassen Volcanic National Park. Left: Bighorn sheep, wild and beautiful in their home environment, Lava Beds National Monument. Pages 76 and 77: Burney Creek drops 132 feet (40.23 meters) over a lava ledge in McArthur-Burney Falls State Park.

Snow geese bide winter time at the Tule Lake National Wildlife Refuge.
Left: Mount Shasta and its satellite Shastina, volcanic giant of the
South Cascades lend a haunting mood to the dawn sky.

Brilliant glow of the snow plant signals the advent of spring by
popping out through the forest duff when late snowpack has melted
away. Left: Early May dogwood blooms cascade in front of Mt. Shasta.

The imposing snow cap of 14,162 foot (4,317 meters) Mount Shasta
looms above the forested Cascades from Herd Peak. Left: Subterranean lava
tube hints of a once fiery volcanic glow, Lava Beds National Monument.

Eagle Falls tumbles into Emerald Bay and Lake Tahoe. Right: Granite
rocks dot the turquoise waterscape of Lake Tahoe from Nevada shores.

A quiet still shrouds the peaceful morning air in view of Donner
Lake and summit. Right: A windswept Sierra juniper thrusts limbs
eastward along the crest of the Sierra Nevada Range in Carson Pass. Pages
88 and 89: Calm prevails over the granite strewn shores of Lake Tahoe.

Leopard lily and lupine blooms lend a splash of color along the
upper San Joaquin river. Left: Barren granite north face of Thompson
Ridge looms above Blue Lake in John Muir Wilderness, Sierra-Nevada range.

Winter's frosted landscape warms under the rays of sunrise on
Lake Tahoe's north shore at Tahoe City, Sierra Nevada Range.

Whitebark root system design in John Muir Wilderness. Left: Sunrise calm and false hellebore, Thousand Island Lake, Minarets Wilderness.

Horse Creek Falls and granite north face of the Cleaver, Minarets
Wilderness. Right: Stonecrop on a granite wall, Feather River Canyon.

Summer travelers enjoy frolicking in Hot Creek on east slope of the Sierra
Nevada Range. Left: Mount Morrison's north face holds Convict Lake at its base.

Moonset and "The Range of Light," eastside from the Owens Valley.

Sculptured ghost of a bristlecone pine weathers another storm in
Patriarch Grove of the White Mountains. Left: Massive ramparts of 12,590 foot
(3,837 meters) Mt. Conness dominates Sierra Nevada Range above
Tenaya Lake and glacial boulders, Olmsted Point, Yosemite National Park.

"Half Dome was probably the first of the Yosemite rocks to
emerge from the ice burnished and glowing like a crystal"... John Muir.
Left: An autumn morning dawns over Half Dome in Yosemite Valley.

Apple blossoms and Half Dome make spring a delightful spectacle
in Yosemite Valley. Right: El Capitan above gentle flow of Merced River.

Light of dawn touches the tops of Mount Ritter and Mount Banner
reflecting in Garnet Lake, Minarets Wilderness. Lelt: Sierra juniper, Carson Pass.

The Sierra crest of Mount Humphreys, Basin Mountain and Mount Tom
silhouette a clearing storm from an evening sky above Bishop. Right: Jeffery
pine in twilight atop Sentinel Dome, Yosemite National Park.

An infinite sky reflects in a quiet pool of Yosemite Valley. Left: Lower
Yosemite Falls makes a 320 foot (97.54 meters) drop in Yosemite Creek, with
the 1,430 foot (435.86 meters) Upper Yosemite Falls still above in the mist.

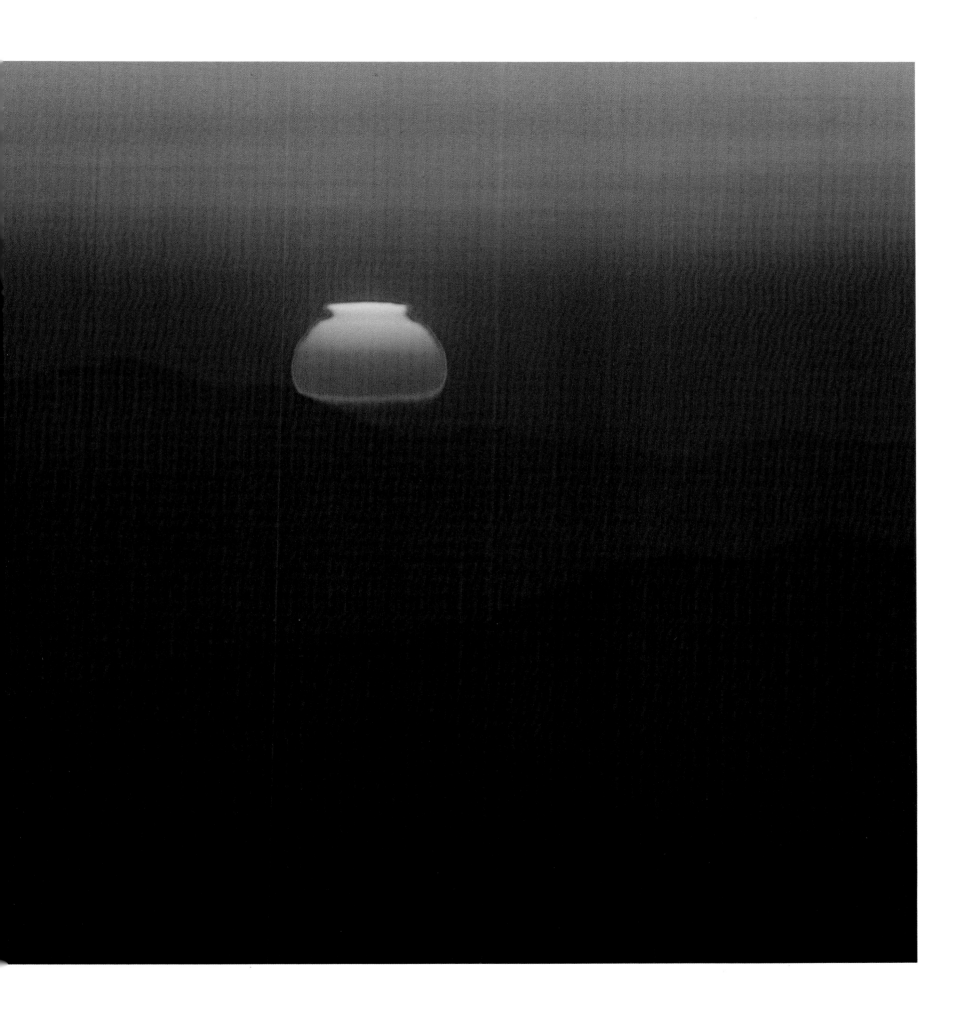

The glowing orb of our sun and forested ridges of the Sierra Nevada.
Left: A November snow decorates fir trees in Sequoia National Park.

Sierra Nevada ridges recede away into the distant San Joaquin Valley
from Moro Rock. Right: The brilliant red mark trunks of the world's largest
trees, sequoias in the Senate Grove, Sequoia National Park.

The majestic winter facade of 12,260 foot (3,737 meters) Mount
Morrison on the Sierra Nevada eastside. Left: Fog cloaks the Sequoiadendron
giganteum, moving the eye skyward close to 300 feet (91.44 meters),
Sequoia National Park.

An autumn transition of cottonwoods in the Owens Valley below
Mt. Langley, Mt. Corcoran and Lone Pine Peak, Sierra Nevada eastside.

A quiet but living spirit lingers in gold mining camp of Bodie.
Right: Weathered wood of a leaning facade and church typify the arrested
decay of Bodie as a California State Park. Pages 124 and 125: April
storm clouds brood over Golden Canyon, Death Valley National Monument.

Bizarre tufa formations emerge from the receding waters along
south shore of Mono Lake near Lee Vining. Left: Dried pods of the desert
trumpet and mud cracks in a dry lake below sea level, Mojave Desert.

Large spread of yellow cups, a member of the evening primrose family,
along the Beatty road in Death Valley National Monument. Left: November frost
high above Mojave Desert on bristlecone roots, White Mountains.

Beavertail cacti blooms decorate an alluvial wash in the Grapevine
Mountains. Right: An inert sand wave appears to crest in the Mesquite Flat
dunes of Death Valley National Monument. Pages 132 and 133:
Timeless sand ripples lead eastward to the Grapevine Mountains.

Desert Bighorn Sheep in the Santa Rosa Mountains. Left: Mesquite
Flat dunes, Death Valley National Monument. Pages 136 and 137: Dawn flushes
14,496 foot (4,418 meters) Mount Whitney, California's highest peak.

Winter clouds envelope Lone Pine Peak above desert rocks in the
Alabama Hills. Left: Sunrise reflections of 11,049 foot (3,368 meters)
Telescope Peak in pool at Badwater 280 feet (85.34 meters) below sea level.

Teddy bear cholla colony in dawn flush of light, Joshua Tree
National Monument. Left: Clay slopes in Golden Canyon, Death Valley.

Spring winds whip sands across Kelso dunes, Mojave Desert.
Right: Interplay of sun, clouds and joshua, Joshua Tree National Monument.

Winter storm transforms a lone joshua and granite rock into a quiet
fantasy, Joshua Tree National Monument. Left: Patches of phlox mat forest at
8,500 feet (2,591 meters) on El Toro Peak, Santa Rosa Mountains.

Smoke tree lines a desert wash below ridges of the Coxcomb Mountains,
Joshua Tree National Monument. Right: Washingtonia filifera palms
line desert cascade along Palm Canyon trail near Palm Springs.

146

Forested islands above the Colorado Desert, Santa Rosa Mountains.
Left: Primrose thrive in the sands of Anza Borrego Desert State Park.

Evening light touches jumbled array of concretions in the Pumpkin
Patch of Anza Borrego badlands. Right: Forested El Toro Peak lends stark
contrast to sands carpeted with sand verbena in Anza Borrego
Desert State Park. Pages 152 and 153: Haze dissolves the ridges of 10,805 foot
(3,293 meters) Mount San Jacinto high above Palm Springs.

Mojave yucca blooms and Mount San Jacinto in spring entourage.
Right: Coachella Valley date crops (above) and rows of strawberries (lower).

Pages 156 and 157: Washingtonia filifera palms group around an ancient desert
spring at 1000 Palms Oasis, snow frosted Santa Rosa Mountains on the horizon.

Palm fronds drape over a jungle of granites and the creek in Andreas Canyon. Left: The low waters of a desert creek wander through truck size boulders in Palm Canyon belonging to the Agua Caliente Indians.

A brisk air and drifting cumulus stimulate boys into a playful run
along the south coast near Laguna Beach. Left: Fresh mantle of snow blankets
pines and dome housing 200 inch Stellar telescope on Mt. Palomar.

San Diego skyline and eucalyptus from Balboa Park. Right: Mission
San Diego de Alcala, founded in 1769 by Franciscan Padre Junipero Serra.

Storm clearing over the normally mild mannered La Jolla coastline
of coves and beach strands. Right: Winter surf and Pacific headlands.

Fountain doubles image of adobe facade at San Luis Rey. Left: Bell tower
of Mission San Luis Rey de Francia near Oceanside. Pages 168 and 169:
Late glow of winter's evening over Los Angeles from Mount Wilson.

Frenzied traffic flows along Harbor freeway in downtown Los Angeles. Right:
Frosted Jeffery pine lends an icy window for 10,004 foot (3,049 meters) Mount
San Antonio (Old Baldy), San Gabriel range in a mid April storm.

Lofty ridges of 10,805 foot (3,293 meters) Mount San Jacinto
distill with the afternoon haze and smog from Los Angeles basin.
From the top of El Toro Peak, Santa Rosa Mountains.

Arms of lone joshua reach for the ethereal light of an evening sun
in Antelope Valley near Palmdale. Pages 174 and 175: Channel Islands
above tidal pools off the coast of Santa Barbara.

Gilia and lupine dust foothills of the Tehachapi Mountains.
Right: Meadow of wild tidy-tips surround oaks in the San Rafael Mountains.

In 1786 Father Fermin Lasuen established Mission Santa Barbara,
often called "Queen of the Missions." Right: Upper Mission Creek in the
foothills of the coastal Santa Ynez Mountains behind Santa Barbara.

June winds sweep coastal fog inland toward San Luis Obispo from
above Morro Bay. Right: Summer wild flowers and fog tableau below the
Santa Lucia Mountains, Big Sur coastline north of Point Sur.

Last light of a summer day flickers through a valley oak in Santa
Ynez Valley. Right: A milling stone and facade at the Mission San Antonio.

Nostalgic fishing seaport at Morro Bay. Right: Ocean waters ebb
and flow around tidal tableau of starfish and seastacks, north coast.

Upper Yosemite Falls cascades 1,430 feet (435.86 meters) freefall above cowparsnip, Yosemite Valley. Right: Benign world of granite greet the alpine hiker from top of 14,042 foot (4,280 meters) Mount Langley. Sierra crest to Mount Whitney straddles Sequoia Park and the John Muir Wilderness.

Lightning scarred Jeffery pine overlooks the maze of glacially
formed domes and peaks from its mighty perch on Sentinel Dome. Right:
Upper middle fork San Joaquin River, Mount Ritter and Mount
Banner below Thousand Island Lake in the Minarets Wilderness.

Spring storm clouds veil Half Dome above the granite staircase of
the Merced River with Vernal and Nevada Falls in Yosemite Valley. Left: An
autumn fog shrouds sequoia trunks, Sequoia National Park.